Let's Investigate Plastic Pollution

On Land and in the Oceans

by Ruth Owen

With thanks to
Dr. Laura Foster
Head of Clean Seas
Marine Conservation Society

Published in 2019 by Ruby Tuesday Books Ltd.

Copyright © 2019 Ruby Tuesday Books Ltd.

All rights reserved. No part of this publication may be reproduced in whole or in part, stored in any retrieval system, or transmitted in any form or by any means, electronic, mechanical, photocopying, recording, or otherwise, without written permission from the publisher.

Editor: Mark J. Sachner
Designer: Emma Randall
Production: John Lingham

Photo credits:
Alamy: 20 (bottom), 22 (top), 27 (bottom); Cosmographics: 17 (top); Evoware: 29 (top right), 29 (center); FLPA: 21, 30–31; Getty Images: 26; Istock Photo: 23 (bottom); Nature Picture Library: 5 (top), 11 (top); OceanwideImages/Gary Bell: 16 (top); Ruby Tuesday Books: 13, 14, 18; Shutterstock: Cover, 1–2, 4, 5 (bottom), 6–7, 8–9, 10, 11 (bottom), 12, 15, 17 (bottom), 19, 20 (top), 22 (bottom), 23 (top), 24–25, 27 (top), 28, 29 (top left), 31 (bottom); Skipping Rocks Lab: 29 (bottom); WashedAshore.org: 30 (bottom).

Library of Congress Control Number: 2018906353

Print (Hardback) ISBN 978-1-78856-046-7
Print (Paperback) ISBN 978-1-78856-124-2
eBook ISBN 978-1-78856-047-4

Printed and published in the United States of America

For further information including rights and permissions requests, please contact our Customer Service Department at 877-337-8577.

Contents

A Plastic Problem 4
What Is Plastic? 6
Single-Use Plastic 8
Why Is Plastic a Problem? 10
Plastics in Landfills 12
Plastic in the Ocean 14
On the Move! 16
Microplastics 18
Animals in Danger 20
Let's Recycle It 22
Plastic Free 24
Clean Up the Ocean 26
Plastic-Free Packaging 28
Be a Plastic-Free Champion 30
Glossary, Index 32

Words shown in **bold** in the text are explained in the glossary.

The download button shows that there are free worksheets or other resources available. Go to:
www.rubytuesdaybooks.com/getstarted

A Plastic Problem

We all use plastic every day. Some plastic objects make our lives safer or more fun.

Plastic helmet

Plastic soccer ball

But sometimes plastic is used to make things we don't actually need.

Plastic net

The BIG problem with plastic is that when people throw it away, it doesn't disappear.

In fact, almost every piece of plastic that's ever been made is still on Earth somewhere.

When plastic is thrown away, it often ends up in the ocean.

Seal pups playing with plastic

Up to 14.5 million tons (13 million tonnes) of plastic enters the world's oceans each year. That's the same as a dump truck of garbage every minute of every day!

Scientists estimate that 9 out of 10 seabirds have plastic in their stomachs.

It's time to solve the problem of plastic **pollution**, and everyone can help!

What Is Plastic?

Plastic is a material that's produced in factories. It is made from oil, coal, gas, **chemicals**, and other materials.

Plastic objects can be made in any shape or color.

A polyester soccer shirt

Some fabrics, such as polyester, are made from plastics.

Nurdles

These tiny beads are pellets of plastic, known as **nurdles**. In factories, the pellets are heated and melted. Then the melted plastic can be shaped into different objects.

Plastic can be used to make long-lasting parts for computers, cars, and planes.

Car seats and seatbelts contain plastic.

It can even be used to make plastic bones for people who have been badly injured.

However, not all plastic objects are made to be used again and again.

Let's Talk

What kinds of plastic objects do you think might only be used for a short time?

7

Single-Use Plastic

Many plastic objects are made to be used once and then thrown away. They are called single-use plastics.

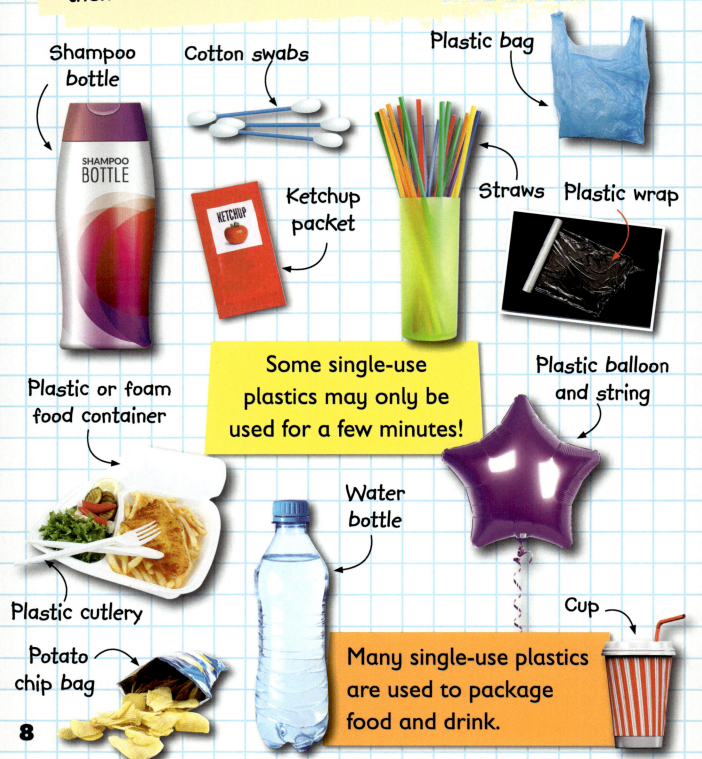

Shampoo bottle

Cotton swabs

Plastic bag

Ketchup packet

Straws

Plastic wrap

Plastic or foam food container

Some single-use plastics may only be used for a few minutes!

Plastic balloon and string

Plastic cutlery

Water bottle

Cup

Potato chip bag

Many single-use plastics are used to package food and drink.

Foods such as potatoes and apples have protective skins. However, many stores sell these foods wrapped in plastic that has to be thrown away.

Let's Talk

Why do you think some stores sell potatoes and apples packaged in single-use plastic?

Let's Explore!

Check out the plastic in your home or classroom.

Can you find the following plastic objects?

- 3 things that are made to be used again and again.
- 3 things that are single use and will soon be thrown away.

Why Is Plastic a Problem?

A piece of single-use plastic is sometimes used for just a few hours. But after it's thrown away, it may be around forever!

If you bury an apple in the ground, it **biodegrades**, or rots away, in a few months.

A biodegrading apple

If you bury a plastic bottle in the ground, it doesn't biodegrade.

In time, a plastic bottle may crack and crumble, but it will still exist as tiny pieces.

Most of the plastic we throw away is still out there somewhere, polluting our world!

Plastic bottles on the ocean floor

Be a Scientist!

Let's investigate how materials biodegrade in soil.

Gather your equipment:
- An apple core
- A small piece of cardboard
- A small piece of thin plastic
- A small trowel
- 3 large pebbles
- A waterproof marker
- A small patch of garden soil
- A notebook and pen

1. Write the words Apple, Cardboard, and Plastic on the three pebbles with the marker.

2. Dig three small holes about 4 inches (10 cm) deep in the soil and put one material in each.

3. Fill in the holes and place a pebble on top to mark the spot. Leave the materials buried for four weeks.

How do you think each material will look after four weeks? Record your predictions in your notebook.

4. After four weeks, dig up your materials.

Did your predictions match what happened?

If you wish, you can bury your materials again to see what happens next.

(At the end of the experiment, dig up the plastic and **recycle** it or throw it away.)

11

Plastics in Landfills

When people throw away plastic, it can end up in a **landfill**.

A landfill is a big hole in the ground where garbage is buried.

Many wild animals visit landfills to find food. Sometimes they get tangled in plastic garbage. They may even eat plastic, thinking it's food.

What Happens at a Landfill?

Trucks collect garbage and take it to a landfill.

The garbage is buried in the ground.

Thick plastic sheets are laid in the hole to keep the garbage from polluting the soil.

Layers of soil

In a landfill, plastics and other kinds of garbage release chemicals that mix with rainwater.

If the protective plastic sheets in the hole split, **toxic** liquids can soak into the soil.

Then this pollution may trickle under the ground and flow into streams, rivers, and the ocean.

Let's Talk

How do you think plastic that's thrown away ends up in the ocean?

Plastic in the Ocean

Billions of plastic objects are polluting our oceans. How did they get there?

A Plastic Bottle's Journey

1. A person drops a bottle on the ground.
2. The bottle blows into a river.
3. The bottle floats along the river.
4. The river flows into the sea, and the bottle goes, too!

Garbage that's left on beaches gets blown or washed out to sea.

People on fishing boats throw away plastic fishing lines and nets.

Bottles, straws, and other plastic objects are dropped into the ocean by people on cruise ships and tourist boats.

Drain

Plastic garbage that's dropped in the street may get washed down a drain with rainwater.

The drain leads to a river that will eventually flow into the ocean.

Sometimes, plastic from landfills gets blown into rivers or out to sea.

Things that are flushed down the toilet, such as wipes, may end up in the sea. Wipes should never be flushed away! They can block **sewers**, and many types contain plastic.

Wipe

Plastic packaging

Only three things should be put down the toilet. They all begin with P. What are they?
(The answer is at the bottom of the page.)

Answer: Only pee, poop, and paper should be flushed down the toilet.

15

On the Move!

A piece of plastic in the ocean may travel thousands of miles. It is carried by movements of water called **currents**.

This is a beach on one of the Cocos Keeling Islands in the Indian Ocean. No one lives here, but the beach is covered with millions of pieces of plastic.

Ocean currents carry garbage to the Cocos Keeling Islands from countries far away.

Ocean currents also carry plastic into huge areas of circling water called gyres.

The plastic gets trapped and forms a giant floating garbage patch.

The Great Pacific Garbage Patch is the biggest.

This world map shows the five main garbage patches.

The water in a garbage patch contains big plastic objects and trillions of tiny pieces of plastic.

Scientists estimate that the plastic in the Great Pacific Garbage Patch weighs the same as 500 jumbo jets!

Plastic from a garbage patch

Let's Talk

Where do you think the tiny pieces of plastic in the ocean come from?

Microplastics

Once a plastic bottle is in the ocean, the seawater and sunlight make the plastic **brittle**.

The bottle starts to **degrade**.

It crumbles into pieces that become smaller …

… and smaller …

… and smaller.

These tiny pieces are called **microplastics**.

Scientists think it will take about 450 years for a plastic bottle to degrade in the ocean.

Seabirds, crabs, squid, fish, and other animals may think microplastics are food and eat them.

Let's Investigate!

Tiny pieces of plastic such as nurdles, microbeads, and glitter are also microplastics.

Nurdles

Microbeads in face scrubs

Glitter

How do you think these microplastics end up in the ocean?

(The answers are at the bottom of the page.)

Plastic may contain toxic chemicals. Scientists have also discovered that microplastics soak up chemicals that are already in the sea. All these poisons go into an animal's body when it eats microplastics.

A Plastic Ocean Food Chain

When animals eat microplastics, they might also take in toxic chemicals. This pollution may then be passed up the food chain!

A person eats tuna.

A big fish, such as a tuna, eats the small fish.

Small fish eat microplastics.

Microplastics

Answers: Nurdles get washed down drains in factories or spill from ships during transportation. Microbeads in face scrubs and pieces of glitter get washed down the drain, go through the sewers, and end up in the ocean.

Animals in Danger

Thousands of ocean animals are hurt and killed by plastic pollution every day!

Animals eat garbage, thinking it's food.

Their stomachs get clogged with plastic.

Then they can't eat real food, and they starve to death.

This plastic bag looks like a jellyfish to a turtle.

Animals may struggle to swim if they get tangled in fishing lines and nets. A whale will drown if it can't swim to the surface to breathe.

This young whale has a fishing line tangled in its mouth.

An albatross family

Sometimes seabirds, such as albatrosses, feed plastic to their chicks. The parent birds think the plastic is food. A chick's stomach gets filled with plastic, and it dies.

Scientists collected all this plastic from the stomachs of dead albatross chicks.

Let's Talk

What do you think we can do to STOP plastic pollution?

Let's Recycle It

Many plastic items don't have to be thrown away. They can be recycled.

At a recycling plant, plastic bottles are washed and shredded.

A plastics recycling plant

Crushed plastic bottles

The shredded plastic is melted and turned into nurdles.

Shredded plastic bottles

The nurdles are made into new plastic things.

Unfortunately, many kinds of single-use plastic aren't recycled.

Plastic wrap

Plastic bag

If plastic is combined with another material, it can be difficult and expensive to recycle it.

The top of this soap bottle can't be recycled because it contains metal.

Even recycled plastic can end up in landfills. A plastic bottle may be recycled as stuffing for a sofa. But once the sofa falls apart, it will be thrown away.

Recycling is a great way to keep lots of plastic from becoming pollution.

But using less plastic is the best idea of all!

Plastic Free

No matter how good we all get at recycling, we still use too much plastic. It's time to find ways to go plastic free.

Fruits and vegetables don't need to be wrapped in plastic.

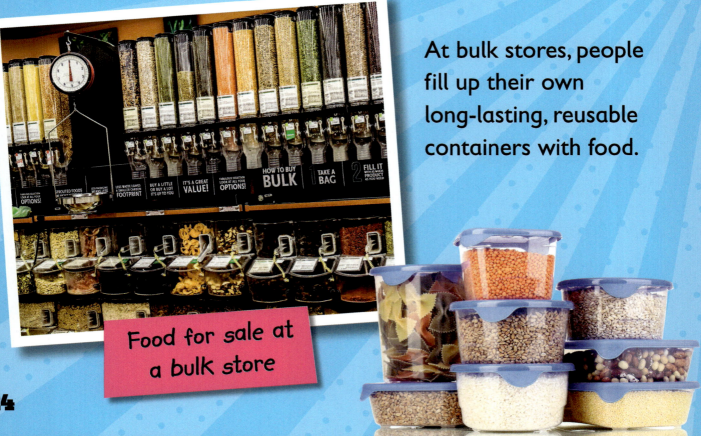

At bulk stores, people fill up their own long-lasting, reusable containers with food.

Food for sale at a bulk store

Plastic-Free Things I Can Do Today!

Feeling thirsty? Fill a glass with water from a tap or use a drinking fountain.

Carry a reusable water bottle when you're on the go.

Say NO to plastic straws!

These straws washed up on a beach.

Remind a grown-up to put leftovers into a reusable container instead of wrapping them in plastic wrap.

If you're choosing a gift for an adult, buy them a reusable shopping bag or coffee cup.

Use a bar of soap instead of bottled soap.

If a store gives you a plastic bag, try to reuse it as many times as possible.

Use a washcloth instead of a wipe.

If you help out with shopping, make plastic-free choices. Glass containers are better than plastic, because glass can be recycled again and again.

25

Clean Up the Ocean

Around the world, many people take part in beach clean-ups. Every piece of plastic that's collected is one less piece in the ocean.

The plastic that's collected from beaches can often be recycled.

Scientists try to figure out where the garbage on a beach came from. If they discover a company has dumped garbage in the sea, the company can be made to stop!

Let's Investigate!

Imagine you are a scientist at a beach clean-up. Carefully observe all the garbage in the picture on page 27.

How many different plastic objects can you spot? Make a list.

Choose one object. How do you think it ended up in the ocean? Draw a picture that shows its journey from being used to being in the sea.

Some beaches are difficult to reach, so it's hard to know what pollution is there.

In Scotland, volunteers in planes fly around the coast.

If they spot plastic pollution in the sea or on a beach, they record it and take photos.

This information can then be used to organize a clean-up.

This garbage washed up on a beach in Scotland.

Plastic-Free Packaging

Scientists and inventors are designing new packaging materials made from plants, seaweed, and mushrooms.

They want to make packaging that will biodegrade, or rot away.

Compost bin

Food and garden waste

Compost

Some people make compost from food and garden waste. The compost is used to feed plants. Some types of biodegradable packaging could be put into compost.

A farmer growing seaweed

Scientists in Indonesia have invented packaging made from seaweed.

This seaweed burger wrapper has no taste and can be eaten with the burger.

Bags made from seaweed

Scientists in London have invented a membrane, or skin, that can hold water.

It is made of seaweed and plants and can be swallowed with the water!

Be a Plastic-Free Champion

If everyone takes small actions, it can have BIG results!

Around the world people are saying NO to single-use plastics such as straws, water bottles, and plastic bags.

Never drop litter! Always recycle trash or put it in a trash can.

Go on a litter hunt or take part in a beach clean-up with your family or friends.

Volunteers for the Washed Ashore Project in the United States clean up beaches. Then the plastic is used to make giant animal sculptures.

A shark sculpture made by Washed Ashore.

Before you buy something plastic, such as a toy, think about the end of its life. Will you be able to pass it on to a friend or give it to a thrift store?

Do one thing and ask your best friend to do it, too. You've just doubled the impact you will have!

Everyone can do something. Let's STOP plastic pollution and save our oceans!

Glossary

biodegrade (bye-oh-dih-GRADE)
To rot away and become part of the environment.

brittle (BRIT-uhl)
Hard but easily breakable.

chemical (KEM-uh-kuhl)
A substance that comes from nature or is made by people. Chemicals can be used to make materials such as plastic.

current (KUR-uhnt)
A movement of water in a stream, river, lake, or ocean.

degrade (dih-GRADE)
To break down or reduce in quality.

landfill (LAND-fil)
A place where large quantities of trash are buried in the ground to get rid of it.

microplastics (mye-kroh-PLAS-tiks)
Tiny pieces of plastic that are less than 0.2 inch (5 mm) long.

nurdles (NURD-uhlz)
Tiny pellets of plastic that are the raw materials for making plastic objects.

pollution (puh-LOO-shun)
Garbage, liquids, gases, or other substances that are harmful to living things and to the land, water, and air.

recycle (ree-SYE-kuhl)
To turn used, old, or unwanted objects and materials into something new.

sewers (SOO-urz)
Large pipes that carry waste from homes and other buildings to treatment plants where the waste is made safe.

toxic (TOK-sik)
Poisonous.

Index

A
animals 5, 12, 18–19, 20–21

B
beach clean-ups 26–27, 30

L
landfills 12–13, 15, 23

N
nurdles 6, 19, 22

O
ocean plastic 5, 13, 14–15, 16–17, 18–19, 20–21

P
plastic bottles 8, 10–11, 14, 18–19, 22–23, 30

plastic-free packaging 28–29

R
recycling 22–23, 24–25, 26, 30

S
sewers 15, 19
single-use plastic 8–9, 10–11, 14–15, 18–19, 23, 24–25, 30